IT'S JUST A BAG, SILLY HORSE

The Adventures of the Healing Herd

Jasmine Chomski

Illustrations by
Carrie Anne Silva

It's Just a Bag, Silly Horse: The Adventures of the Healing Herd
Published by Healing Herd Publications
Toronto, Ontario, Canada

Copyright ©2024, Jasmine Chomski. All rights reserved.

No part of this book may be reproduced in any form or by any mechanical means, including information storage and retrieval systems without permission in writing from the publisher/author, except by a reviewer who may quote passages in a review. All images, logos, quotes, and trademarks included in this book are subject to use according to trademark and copyright laws of the United States of America.

CHOMSKI, JASMINE, Author
IT'S JUST A BAG, SILLY HORSE
JASMINE CHOMSKI

ISBN: 978-1-7382381-0-1, 978-1-7382381-1-8 (paperback)
ISBN: 978-1-7382381-3-2 (hardcover)
ISBN: 978-1-7382381-2-5 (digital)

JUVENILE FICTION / Social Themes / Emotions & Feelings
JUVENILE FICTION / Social Themes / Self-Esteem & Self-Reliance
JUVENILE FICTION / Animals / Horses
JUVENILE FICTION / Lifestyles / Farm & Ranch Life

Illustrations: Carrie Ann Silva
Book Design: Pearly Lim
Editing: Susan Crossman, Crossman Communications
Publishing Management: Susie Schaefer, Finish the Book Publishing

QUANTITY PURCHASES: Schools, companies, professional groups, clubs, and other organizations may qualify for special terms when ordering quantities of this title.
For information, email info@healingherdpublications.com.

All rights reserved by JASMINE CHOMSKI
and HEALING HERD PUBLICATIONS.
This book is printed in Canada.

To the horses, who have been my greatest teachers, and to Turtle, for your unwavering support and faith in me.

Meet the Herd

Sage

Ranger

Takoda

Ali

Meet the Friends

Cali

Jaxson

Angel

Leia

It was another perfect day on the farm.
The sun was shining, the birds were singing, and
the horses were happily munching on the grass.

Everyone felt peaceful and calm.

Until...

Something began blowing across the field.

It whirled and danced in the wind.

It was headed right for the horses!

The horses stopped eating and looked up. They had a feeling that something might be wrong.

As the object moved closer to the horses, Takoda and Ali took off running.

"It's going to eat us!" Ali shouted.

Sage asked, "What is it?"

"I don't know but it's dangerous!" Takoda replied. "Run for your lives!"

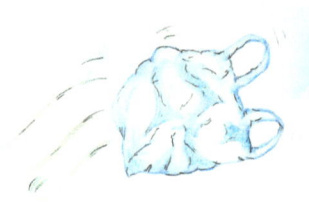

"Run for your lives!"
shouted Sage.

The horses huddled together,
far away from the scary thing.

Jaxson, Leia, and Cali the dog rushed over to see what was going on.
What had scared the horses so badly?

"We almost died!" exclaimed Ranger.

"Thank goodness you're here!" said Ali. "That thing attacked us out of nowhere!"

Jaxson and Leia looked everywhere for the monster that surely must be chasing them.

"Where is it?" asked Leia.

Just as Sage trotted forward to show everyone where the object had landed, the wind picked it up again.

"There it is!" Sage yelled and ran back to join the other horses.

"Why, that's just a plastic bag, silly horse," said Jaxson.

Surely the little human couldn't be right, thought Sage.

Just then the wind settled down and the object stopped moving. The horses went to check it out.

They moved closer to it and then backed away. A little closer, and then away again.

Bit by bit they got closer and closer.

When the object didn't move again, Sage carefully went up, sniffed it and he knew everything was going to be okay.

He turned to the minis and said,
"It's just a bag, silly horse."

The next day Jaxson visited the horses. Sage could tell by his face that he was feeling troubled.

"What's wrong, Jaxson?" Sage asked.

"I'm worried about school starting tomorrow," said Jaxson. "I'm scared. What if I don't like it? What if no one likes me? What if the teacher is mean? What if I don't do well?"

Sage listened closely. He knew how Jaxson felt. Just yesterday, he felt scared when he didn't know what was going on. He was sure the bag was going to eat him, just like Jaxson was sure that going to school wasn't going to be any good at all.

"It's just a thought, silly human," Sage told Jaxson. "And thoughts can't hurt you. Let's talk about this."

"Horses may run away from things at first, but they always come back and investigate," Sage continued. "They need to know if it really is dangerous."

"Is something at school going to eat you?" Sage asked seriously.

"No," said Jaxson.

"Is something at school going to hurt you?"

"No," Jaxson said again.

"Is school a safe place?" Sage continued.

"Yes. There are people there to keep you safe." Jaxson replied.

"Have you ever gone to school before and had fun?" Sage asked.

"Yes." Said Jaxson. "I really have."

"Whenever we think things, we feel some feelings in our body," Sage said. "If you want to feel better, you need to think different thoughts. How do you want to feel when you are at school?"

"I want to feel happy," Jaxson said.

"So, close your eyes and think of a time when you felt happy at school," said Sage. "Feel those feelings in your body."

Jaxson did what Sage asked and he began to feel happy.

"This works!" Jaxson said.

The next day, Jaxson went running to the horses to tell them all about his amazing day at school.

"It was just a thought, silly human," Sage said.
"Of course you had a good day."

And together they went to play with the other horses.

Reflection Questions

1. What's something you feel worried about?

2. What are the feelings you have when you think about it? Make a list of feeling words.

3. Where do you feel those feelings in your body?

4. How do you want to feel about this situation?

5. Can you close your eyes and feel those feelings?

About the author
Jasmine Chomski

Photo Credit: HorseTouchLifeDesign

Once a little girl wishing for a horse, Jasmine Chomski now leads a herd of ten incredible healing horses, drawing inspiration and wisdom from their presence. As a devoted psychotherapist, she pours her heart into aiding adults in healing their inner child and teaching children how to become healthy, strong adults.

At the core of it all is Jasmine's mission – an unwavering commitment to empowering individuals to handle life with strength and resilience. By merging her passion for horses with her dedication to mental health, she's on a quest to enable people to break free from survival and learn to thrive despite life's challenges.

About the Illustrator

A wizard of turning spilled paint into pure magic, Carrie Silva's artistic journey began with doodling on her math homework. When she's not working on enchanting creative projects, she's inspiring kids to embrace their inner artists, or busy being head cowgirl of her own lively herd that includes her son and Whippet sidekick at the family homestead located on the outskirts of Toronto.

Let's continue the adventure beyond the book!

Visit **www.jasminechomski.com** to discover how we can join you on the journey towards a more resilient and empowered life.

Check out online programs and other practical resources designed to support children and parents.

If you're in the area, don't miss the opportunity to meet the horses at our events.

Scan the QR code below for more information.

www.ingramcontent.com/pod-product-compliance
Lightning Source LLC
LaVergne TN
LVHW071029070426
835507LV00002B/83